W9-BTK-776

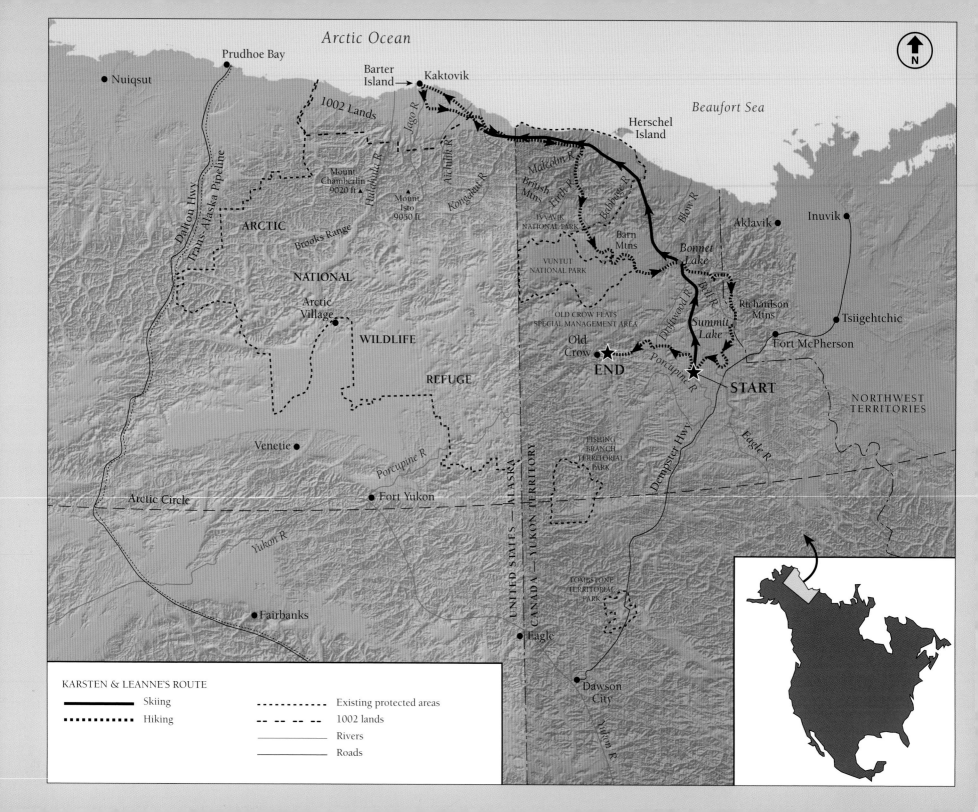

Arctic Ocean

Prudhoe Bay

Nuiqsut

Barter
Island → Kaktovik

Beaufort Sea

1002 Lands

Herschel
Island

Jago R

Hulahula R

Aichilik R

Kongakut R

Mount
Chamberlin
9020 ft ▲

Mount
Isto
9050 ft ▲

Malcolm R

British
Mtns

Firth R

Babbage R

Blow R

Aklavik

Inuvik

Dalton Hwy

Trans-Alaska Pipeline

ARCTIC

Brooks Range

IVVAVIK
NATIONAL PARK

Barn
Mtns

*Bonnet
Lake*

Richardson
Mtns

Tsiigehtchic

NATIONAL

VUNTUT
NATIONAL PARK

Driftwood R

Bell R

*Summit
Lake*

Fort McPherson

Arctic
Village

WILDLIFE

OLD CROW FLATS
SPECIAL MANAGEMENT AREA

Old
Crow

Porcupine R

★ START

REFUGE

★ END

NORTHWEST
TERRITORIES

Venetie

Porcupine R

FISHING
BRANCH
TERRITORIAL
PARK

Dempster Hwy

Eagle R

Arctic Circle

Fort Yukon

Yukon R

UNITED STATES — ALASKA

CANADA — YUKON TERRITORY

Fairbanks

Eagle

TOMBSTONE
TERRITORIAL
PARK

Dawson
City

Tatun R

KARSTEN & LEANNE'S ROUTE

——————— Skiing

••••••••••• Hiking

- - - - - - - - Existing protected areas

– – – – – 1002 lands

——————— Rivers

——————— Roads

N

Contents

CHAPTER ONE

Introduction

My park ranger uniform.

I GREW UP IN CALGARY, a city of half a million people, doing what most city kids do: in winter I played hockey after school; in summer I played soccer and biked around our neighborhood. Every Friday night my parents packed up our car and took my sister and me to the nearby mountains. I loved our time there so much, I decided to become a park ranger when I grew up. That's exactly what I did.

My first few years as a park ranger were spent in the same mountains where I'd grown up. A few years later I got moved north to Ivvavik National Park, right next to the Arctic Ocean and Alaska. It is unlike any place I have ever been. It has no roads, no buildings, or other kinds of human development. It doesn't even have hiking trails. The only trails are those that have been carved into the mountains by a huge herd of 123,000 caribou on its way to the Alaskan calving grounds. It's an amazing migration across four mountain ranges and dozens of rivers that they've been making for the last 27,000 years.

Threats to those Alaskan calving grounds are why my new wife, Leanne, and I decided to follow the caribou for five months. The very spot where they give birth—a place called the Arctic National Wildlife Refuge—is being eyed by oil companies for the oil that exists underneath it. Geologists say there's enough oil to fuel America for six months to a year. Economists and oil executives say extracting it will generate millions of dollars and hundreds of jobs. The caribou haven't had any say at all.

Leanne and I wanted to change that. By trekking alongside the animals and filming and photographing their epic migration, we hoped to tell their side of the story. The importance of the calving grounds can't be counted in dollars and cents; it is in all they endure to get there and back each year. The hundreds of miles across mountain ranges and rivers. The wolf chases. The grizzly bears, the blizzards, and the bugs. This is the story that needs to be told.

Above: By following the caribou and their trails, Leanne and I hoped to tell their story.

Right: Caribou swim one of dozens of rivers on their epic migration to the calving grounds.

Following caribou would sometimes mean traveling through the night.

As far as we knew, no one had ever tried to follow a herd of caribou for five months, and for good reason. For one thing, the animals are highly unpredictable. One year they follow one mountain range to the calving grounds, the next year another. And sometimes they switch partway. To follow caribou would mean not knowing where we were going ahead of time. Every decision of every day—right down to when we would eat, where we would camp, how long we would sleep—would depend on the animals.

It was hard not to get discouraged as we began to get ready. We learned that caribou could cover 90 miles (145 kilometers) a day! And, unlike us, they didn't need to carry heavy packs full of supplies. Their wide, paddlelike hooves acted like snowshoes in the deep, soft snow. Their coats of hollow hair insulated them from the worst Arctic blizzards. And when it came time to eat, they would simply nibble at the lichens, shrubs, and bits of grass.

What Leanne and I did have, however, was experience. Together we had climbed some of the highest mountains in Central and North America. We had also walked and skied through the Rocky Mountains for one and a half years. We knew following caribou would be harder than any of those expeditions, but we knew we would be strong as long as we stayed together.

It was for these very reasons that we got married just before leaving. We were going to honeymoon with the herd.

Above: Leanne sorts and packages five months of dried food.

Left: Our wedding portrait, taken two months before following the caribou.

7

CHAPTER TWO
Setting Off

IT WAS EARLY APRIL and still cold and snowy in the Arctic when we got a phone call from a friend living in the village of Old Crow, Yukon. People were hunting caribou, he told us. The spring migration was on.

There is no road to Old Crow, so we raced to the airport and hopped on a plane. A few hours later we landed in the village. After talking to some of the 300 native Gwich'in people living there, we met Randall Tetlichi. He offered to tow us up the frozen Porcupine River on his snowmobile to look for caribou. People said he was a good hunter. If caribou were out there, he would find them.

Sixty miles (100 kilometers) later, he did.

Right: Randall Tetlichi along the frozen Porcupine River.

Left: The snowy tundra and one of four mountain chains crossed by the caribou, as seen from the plane.

Randall hunting caribou just as his father, grandfather, and great-grandfather did.

Before I could admire the animals' beauty, they were running. Randall had jumped off his snowmobile with his rifle.

At first I was shocked by the shots, but then I remembered the prices in the village grocery store in Old Crow. A beef steak that cost $5 where Leanne and I had grown up was $20 there.

But it was more than to save money that Randall hunted. It was his tradition. His father had hunted caribou, his grandfather before that, and every Gwich'in man before him for thousands of years. He told us that if he didn't hunt, he would lose his way in life.

That night Randall told us stories and offered advice for the trip ahead. He told us of a time when people could talk to caribou and caribou could talk to people. Then he told us to pay attention to our dreams. I thanked him for his stories and advice but didn't believe them. I was a scientist and park ranger. As far as I was concerned, they were just legends and myths.

Members of the Porcupine caribou herd flee Randall's bullets.

Leanne and Randall hug good-bye on the ice and snow of the Porcupine River.

The groups of caribou that fled Randall's bullets were long gone by the next morning, but Leanne and I decided it was time to start anyway. We had talked about following caribou long enough; it was time to actually do it. We found a well-trodden caribou trail that went north from the river, then turned to say good-bye.

"Well, I guess we'll see you in the fall," I said to Randall as I clipped on my skis. I was worried and scared about the months of wilderness travel that lay ahead, but I put on a brave face.

"Yeah," he said matter-of-factly. "I guess we'll see you in the fall."

Left: Leanne on one of the well-trodden caribou trails heading north from the Porcupine River.

CHAPTER THREE

Spring Migration

IT WAS FIVE DAYS before we saw our first animal. Five days of trudging along the narrow, slippery snow trench with heavy packs digging into our shoulders. We couldn't ski along it—the snow was too deep and the path left by the caribou too tight. Instead we stepped from packed hoof print to packed hoof print, balancing as though we were on a narrow log. One misstep to the side and we landed headfirst in the soft, deep snow.

That exhausting routine continued until we broke out of the trees on the fifth day. There the snow had been packed by the winter winds and could support our skis. We could move faster. The caribou trail grew fresher. Then, as we climbed into the first chain of mountains, we saw them: a line of far-off shapes climbing to the top of a high, snowy ridge.

Left: Our first view of caribou migrating through the Richardson Mountains, Yukon.

Right: Climbing through deep snow carrying all our equipment was exhausting.

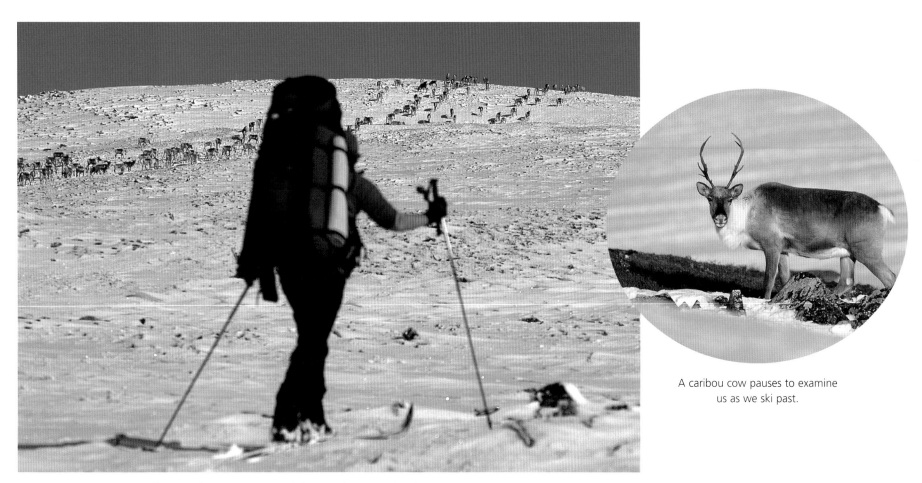

A caribou cow pauses to examine us as we ski past.

Leanne follows a few hundred yards (a few hundred meters) behind the migrating caribou.

As long as we kept 100 to 200 yards (90 to 180 meters) away, the animals didn't seem to mind us. Of course, they stopped and looked when we appeared around a corner or over a ridge, but never for long. And why would they? We weren't moving fast or chasing them. We didn't have guns. After staring a few seconds, the caribou simply plodded on.

They did react, however, when three wolves appeared a day later, the first of many we would see in the coming months. Every caribou stopped and stood at full attention, snorting and huffing and pawing at the snow. When the wolves edged closer, every caribou took a step back and began to run.

As the caribou ran off, every one of the thousands of animals veered and turned in perfect time as if controlled by a single brain. It was like watching a school of fish or a flock of birds moving over the snowdrifts. With so many choices the wolves got confused, chasing one animal and then another, unable to make up their minds. Each time they hesitated, the caribou pulled a little farther ahead. Finally the wolves gave up.

The nights were still cold, but the days were getting warmer, melting the snow and exposing the grass and lichens underneath. As some caribou stopped to feed, Leanne and I pulled past them on skis. Migrating with the herd wasn't going to be as tough as we first thought.

As soon as we thought that, however, the first blizzard struck. The wind and blowing snow were so powerful, we couldn't stand—never mind ski. Pulling the tent from our packs, we wrestled the poles into the snapping, flapping fabric, then struggled to climb in.

The storm was nothing like the ones we'd experienced farther south. With each hard gust it threatened to rip and shred our tent. We shivered inside as the sunny mountains turned white around us, and we wondered if the storm would erase us as well. But then half a dozen shadows drifted toward us. Leanne and I looked out a crack in the tent door, then at each other. Caribou! Not only were they out in the driving snow, but they were feeding! For the caribou it was just another day.

Above: Reindeer lichen—one of the caribou's favorite foods.

Right: I poke my head out of the snowy, icy tent after one of many storms.

Ghost-like caribou move through the blowing snow of an Arctic storm.

I wade through one of dozens of icy rivers behind the caribou.

As the weeks went by, we learned to accept the blizzards, the long days of climbing up and down mountains, and, with the creeks and rivers beginning to thaw, the icy-cold wades. What was harder to accept, however, was when the hungry grizzly bears came out of their dens after a winter of hibernating.

At first none of the bears bothered us, but then one followed our ski track for 2 miles (3 kilometers) and walked in as we pitched camp. We waved our arms. We shouted. We even set off a couple of fire crackers, but nothing worked. The bear continued to circle around us, smacking its lips.

What finally pushed the bear off was when I lifted the whole tent above my head and lunged toward it. I looked big and strange enough for the bear to be scared away. Leanne and I were scared too. Really scared. That night we talked about quitting.

In the end, though, we didn't quit. After a month of skiing, we were too close to the calving grounds to give up. Besides, the caribou weren't stopping despite the blizzards, bears, and wolves. I looked at their bulging stomachs and felt ashamed for even thinking of giving up. Despite being pregnant, the cows continued on without complaint.

A hungry grizzly bear following the caribou to their calving grounds.

Caribou cows wait to give birth on Alaska's coastal plain in the exact place where oil companies want to drill.

CHAPTER FOUR

Calving

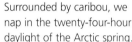

AFTER SIX WEEKS AND 400 MILES (640 kilometers) of skiing and climbing across mountains and rivers, we finally reached the calving grounds. We heard grunts, snorts, and clicking tendons all around us, mixed with the sound of teeth clipping and chewing grass. Hundreds, if not thousands, of expectant mothers surrounded us, making us hostages in the tent. Unlike during the spring migration, just the sight of our heads poking out the door was enough to spook the caribou. We had to stay put until they were done giving birth.

Surrounded by caribou, we nap in the twenty-four-hour daylight of the Arctic spring.

It was hard not to go a little crazy in such cramped quarters. Everything Leanne and I did in the tiny space—whether it was cooking, eating, taking photographs, even going to the bathroom—meant bumping each other with elbows or knees. And then there was the smell. Neither of us had taken a shower in more than six weeks! But we couldn't escape the tent.

By the time the caribou have crossed dozens of thawing rivers to arrive at their calving grounds, most of their predators have been left behind.

It made sense to us that the mothers would be so skittish. They can't run from danger while they give birth and tend to their young. This is why they migrate so far: to separate themselves from the wolves, who den and raise their own offspring back in the mountains, and other predators, who stay further south.

Another reason the calving grounds are so valuable is because of the lack of insects there. The cooler temperatures along the Arctic Ocean delay the hatching of mosquitoes and biting flies by a few weeks — just long enough for a cow to give birth and bond with its calf.

The special kind of cotton grass that grows only on the calving grounds.

Finally there is food. The 20-mile (30-kilometer)-wide strip of coastal plain is the only place in the caribou's range where a certain kind of protein-rich cotton grass grows. It's the perfect meal for a skinny mother trying to produce milk for her hungry, growing calf.

A cow and calf feed undisturbed by bugs that have already hatched deeper in the mountains.

A caribou cow minutes after giving birth just outside our tent.

It was only after three days of being surrounded by caribou that Leanne and I actually saw a calf being born. The mother lay down and started grunting in time with the contractions that gripped her belly. A minute later she pushed out a tiny, wet bundle in one smooth heave.

The new mother didn't pause long to admire her baby. Within five minutes, the calf took its first step. Half an hour later, it was walking smoothly. By the end of the first day, it ran circles across the lumpy tundra, frolicking and jumping with the other calves while the mothers, in turn, frolicked and jumped back. It was the first time Leanne and I had seen adult caribou be so playful, and we couldn't help but laugh from inside the tent as caribou charged and chased all around.

Within minutes of being born, the calf can stand and drink its mother's milk.

Such playing strengthened the calf-mother bond. No sooner was a calf running away than the cow called it back. Each mother had a unique grunt, each calf a particular bleat, and they practiced them over and over. How well they learned and responded to each other's calls would determine whether the calves survived. Ahead were tough climbs, wolf chases, and stampedes to flee the bugs. If the cows and calves weren't well bonded, they would lose each other and the calves would surely die.

After only ten days, the window of opportunity to bond and grow strong on the relatively safe calving grounds began to close. With each passing day, more and more bugs drifted through the warming air. Soon there would be swarms of them.

Above: A cow prepares to leave the calving grounds, followed by its calf.

Left: A calf returns after recognizing its mother's unique grunts.

Groups of cow and calf caribou race off the calving grounds, back toward the mountains.

CHAPTER FIVE

Post Calving

AFTER TEN DAYS of sitting and watching the newborn calves play around our tent, Leanne and I suddenly sprang into action. The caribou were leaving. The wobbly-legged calves of just a few days before were running after their mothers, who were racing for the mountains. Leanne and I shook the stiffness out of our legs and hobbled after them, worrying once again about being left behind.

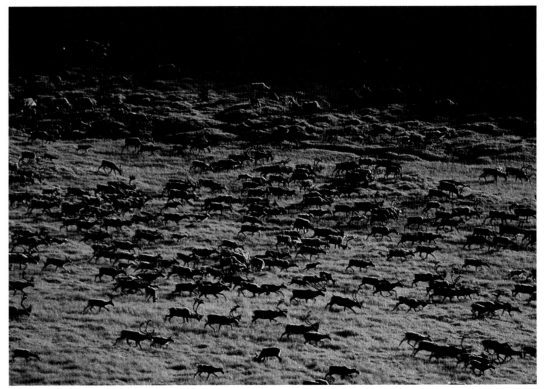

Calves gallop after their trotting mothers as the herd flees the calving grounds.

A caribou cow buries her head in the moss, trying to escape the pain of bot flies burrowing up her sensitive snout.

It was the bugs that forced the caribou to swarm off the coastal plain. Millions of mosquitoes had arrived and they chased the caribou in clouds that sucked a cup of blood from an animal per day!

But it wasn't just the mosquitoes that bothered the animals: the bot and warble flies were hatching too. No bigger than houseflies, they could inflict tremendous damage. The bot flies burrowed up the caribou's noses to lay their eggs, and the warble flies bored holes through their skin. No wonder the caribou were galloping. No wonder they no longer cared whether Leanne and I were hidden or in the open. The bugs had changed everything. All that mattered now was how fast the caribou could get to the mountains and find a brisk ridgetop wind.

Leanne and I had easier ways to keep the bugs at bay. We wore long-sleeved shirts, long pants, and mesh hoods that the bugs couldn't sting through, and once we zipped the doors shut and squashed all the mosquitoes that came in with us, we had a bug-free refuge in the tent. Not that we ever used it for long—the caribou wouldn't allow it. Unlike during the spring migration, they weren't stopping. They raced for the mountains both day and night.

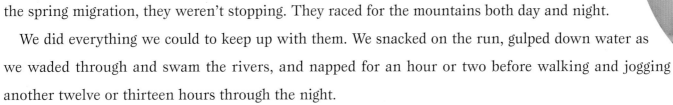

We did everything we could to keep up with them. We snacked on the run, gulped down water as we waded through and swam the rivers, and napped for an hour or two before walking and jogging another twelve or thirteen hours through the night.

Above: We were thankful for bugproof clothing as mosquitoes swarm Leanne's back.

Left: Walking through the night, we tried to fool our bodies into doing more with less.

33

But the pace, along with the hundreds of miles (hundreds of kilometers) we'd already covered, had taken a toll. We began to stumble. We became dizzy and disoriented. And, after months of eating nothing but dried food, our bodies began burning muscle instead of fat. But the caribou were oblivious to such limits. It was as if fatigue and hunger didn't affect them. They climbed off the coastal plain and surged into the foothills, moving from one valley to the next valley as if gravity didn't exist.

Leanne and I kept pushing after the animals, running as much as we could with the heavy packs, stumbling under the weight, no longer knowing what was day or night. Was it breakfast, lunch, or dinner we were supposed to eat? It didn't matter. We stuffed in handfuls of food and pressed on.

Leanne rests and films as bug-bothered caribou surge through the foothills of the British Mountains.

When we did stop to put something in our mouths, it usually had caribou hair in it. The animals were shedding their winter coats, and their hair was everywhere—on our clothes, in our sleeping bag, in our food, and in the water we drank in the creeks.

And then it happened: the thing that Randall had told us to watch out for when we'd said our good-byes two months earlier. In our exhausted and hungry state we began having visions. The line between being caribou and being human shifted. The animals talked to us through our dreams.

Above: Leanne inspects one of millions of clumps of caribou hair littering the land.

Left: After the lack of sleep and rest, the boundary between the waking and dream world began to blur.

CHAPTER SIX

Summer

THE FIRST DREAM was about a bull caribou with big velvety antlers, walking along a green ridge studded with boulders. Behind it rose a sea of gray peaks. I described it to Leanne when we woke from one of our naps. It was strange; until then it had been only cows and their newborn calves we'd been following. We hadn't seen an adult bull on the whole trip.

Leanne didn't say anything at first. She just looked at me, unzipped the tent door, then climbed out and began to pack up. A few seconds later she was back, pointing for me to look outside the tent, too excited to speak.

There, walking on the next ridge, was a lone bull in the exact scene I'd dreamed.

Left: The caribou even took over my dreams.

Right: My surprising vision come to life.

More bulls joined the herd in the following days, and with them came more dreams. It wasn't just me having them; it was Leanne too. She dreamed of caribou swimming a cliff-lined river. She dreamed of a lone musk ox feeding in the willows. One by one those dreams came true.

What was happening? Had we stepped into a magical world where we could predict the future? Or was it that we were seeing, hearing, and feeling things that had been there but we'd never noticed?

Life with the caribou was so different from life in the city. Without ringing phones, wailing sirens, and the roar of buses to overwhelm us, we were relearning to use our senses. By being caribou we were being more human. We were returning to our wild selves.

Caribou swim the cliff-lined waters of the Firth River, just as one of Leanne's dreams predicted.

Leanne follows the thrumming to another throng of caribou.

One thing we noticed was the thrumming, a low rumbling sound that we could barely hear made by large groups of caribou. It wasn't hooves thundering across the tundra; the sound was deeper and softer—like a melody that we heard through our feet and chests more than through our ears. It sounded like water running over a boulder, or the pluck of a giant, thick string. It was there but not there, vibrating on the edge of human hearing. But we learned to trust it. When we did, it led us to great throngs of caribou wheeling into the wind.

For the rest of July we looped, circled, and wandered through the mountains, following the caribou who were following the shifting winds. When the wind was strong, there was no problem—the animals fed in the grassy valleys as calmly as beef cows in a farmer's field. But as soon as the breeze dropped, a panic broke out in the herd. Animals bucked and kicked at the flies as they charged across creeks and clambered up rocky slopes to get away.

Some calves got separated from the herd in the chaos and approached us, thinking we were their mothers. At first Leanne and I tried to push them back toward the herd, but it was no use. More often than not, they raced off in the wrong direction until they were nothing but tiny brown specks.

Leanne and I witnessed many such separations and, as the summer wore on, stumbled across the tiny carcasses that showed how they almost always led to death. At first we despaired over these carcasses, but as the weeks passed we began to see the good in it. Parts of each dead body were being carried off by other living things. Big hunks of meat were torn away by eagles and foxes. As we reentered the mountains, the protein-rich organs (heart, kidney, and liver) were consumed by bears and wolves. The cartilage was being pecked away by jaegers and ravens. The calcium-rich bones were gnawed by mice. The soft fur lined many birds' nests.

Above: A lost calf approaches Leanne, wondering if she's its mother.

Left: I hold up a leg from one of many carcasses found along the way.

Opposite: Bulls and cows charge across a creek while calves follow, trying to escape the bugs.

CHAPTER SEVEN

Fall

SEASONS CHANGE abruptly in the Arctic. One day Leanne and I were sweating in the tent with bugs buzzing around us, the next we sat huddled under a tarp trying to get warm.

There were signs of the coming winter: the low-lying bushes were turning yellow and orange. The brown feathers of the ptarmigans were turning white again. But Leanne and I paid little attention to them. Where we came from, it was still summer. August was too early for winter. Yet here we were in the Arctic, shivering in snow.

After four months of following caribou, our clothes hung off our bodies, our cheeks were hollow, and we couldn't get warm.

Left to right: Dwarf birch and willow bushes turn red and yellow around Leanne's feet; Leanne and I seek shelter after an early snowstorm; a ptarmigan midway between its summer and winter plumage.

We probably could have kept walking for another few months if everything went well, but what if it didn't? What if we slipped during one of the many river crossings? What if another hungry grizzly came into our camp? Realizing we didn't have the energy to get ourselves out of a dangerous predicament forced a tough decision: we would begin the fall migration and get back to the village of Old Crow while we still could.

Left: We needed to head south with or without the caribou.

Above: We realized we no longer had the energy to swim big rivers or stave off curious grizzlies.

Small groups of caribou follow us south along the ridges of the Yukon's Richardson Mountains.

After months of following the routes and schedules of the caribou, it seemed strange to pull out a map, plot our route, and follow it regardless of what the animals were doing. We felt like we were abandoning our old friends and teachers. But no sooner had we started south than groups of caribou began to follow us! They weren't big groups—now that the cooler weather had killed off the bugs, there was no need for the caribou to mass together—but they were caribou nonetheless. It was as if they weren't done telling us their story.

For the next four weeks, the caribou escorted us past many of the same spots we'd visited earlier that spring: the place where Leanne and I had been blasted by our first blizzard; the ridge where we'd seen our first wolf chase; and the cabin where Randall had told us stories before saying good-bye. It seemed a lifetime since that night when I'd so doubted what he told us. Now, five months later, I knew it was true. People can talk to caribou and caribou can talk to us.

Green grass and the bleached antlers of a bull caribou mark the place where we experienced our first Arctic blizzard months before.

The last caribou we saw were swimming the Porcupine River just 3 miles (5 kilometers) upstream of the village of Old Crow. It was a small group—three cows and one calf—and we watched as they paddled across the water.

We were near the end of our journey—in another few hours we would take our first hot shower and sleep in our first soft bed in five months, not to mention have all the food we could eat. For the caribou, however, there was no end. After swimming the river they would continue south another few hundred miles (few hundred kilometers) to where the bulls would spar for the right to mate with the females, then press on to where they would spend the cold, dark winter, surviving on nothing but lichens. Then, in another few months, it would be time to move to the calving grounds once again.

Life for the herd was always tough. And the developing of their calving grounds would be the greatest challenge they'll ever face. By telling their story, we hope that this important refuge can be saved.

The last group of caribou we would see on the trip charge into the Porcupine River just a few miles (a few kilometers) from the village of Old Crow.

TO LEARN MORE

Books

Hiscock, Bruce. *The Big Caribou Herd: Life in the Arctic
National Wildlife Refuge.* Honesdale, PA: Boyds Mills
Press, 2003.

Miller, Debbie S. *A Caribou Journey.* Boston: Little,
Brown and Company, 1994.

Web Sites

http://www.beingcaribou.com

http://www.alaskawild.org/ak_kids/ak_kids_CARIBOU.html

http://arctic.fws.gov/caribou.htm

http://www.taiga.net/satellite (Tracks the latest movements of
the Porcupine caribou herd via satellite.)

http://www.oldcrow.ca

DVD

Being Caribou. Directed and written by Leanne Allison and
Diana Wilson. National Film Board of Canada, 2004.

How You Can Help

Write a letter to your senator and congressional representative.
Tell them whether or not they should permit oil development
in the caribou's calving grounds. For names and addresses of
politicians in your state, visit http://www.alaskawild.org/
campaigns_arctic_whatyoucando.html.

First published in the United States of America in 2007 by
Walker Publishing Company, Inc.
Distributed to the trade by Holtzbrinck Publishers

For information about permission to reproduce selections from this book, write to
Permissions, Walker & Company, 175 Fifth Avenue, New York, New York 10010

Library of Congress Cataloging-in-Publication Data
Heuer, Karsten.
  Being caribou : five months on foot with a caribou herd / Karsten Heuer.
    p.   cm.
  Includes bibliographical references.
  ISBN-13: 978-0-8027-9565-6 • ISBN-10: 0-8027-9565-X (hardcover)
  ISBN-13: 978-0-8027-9566-3 • ISBN-10: 0-8027-9566-8 (reinforced)
  1. Grant's caribou—Migration—Yukon Territory—Juvenile literature. 2. Grant's
caribou—Alaska—Arctic National Wildlife Refuge—Juvenile literature. I. Title.
  QL737.U55H48 2007   599.65'8—dc22   2006027651

© 2005. Map from the book *Being Caribou* by Karsten Heuer adapted and reprinted
with permission of the publisher, The Mountaineers, Seattle, WA.

Book design by Alyssa Morris
Visit Walker & Company's Web site at www.walkeryoungreaders.com
Printed in China
2 4 6 8 10 9 7 5 3

INDEX

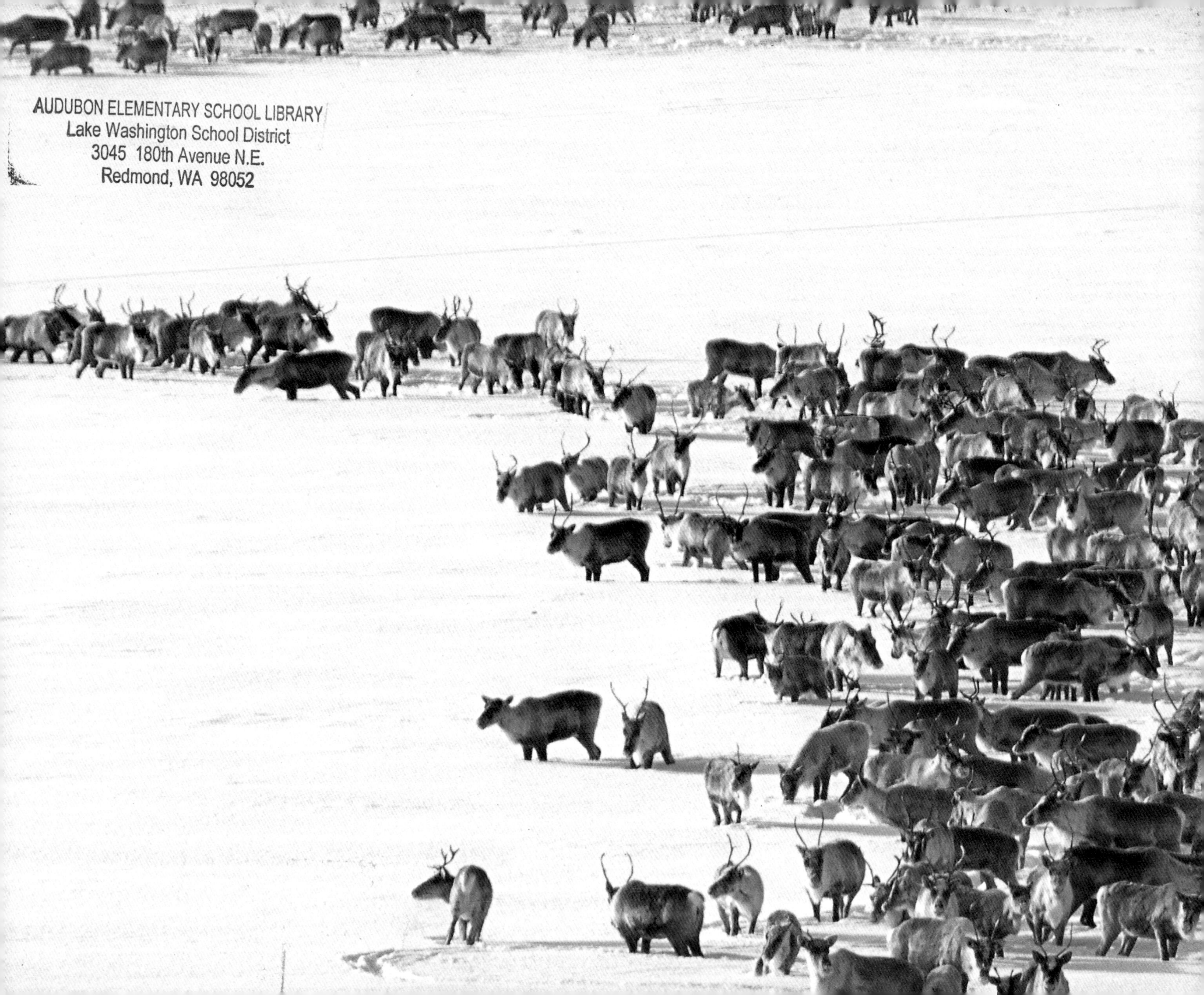